Put Beginning Readers on the Right Track with
ALL ABOARD READING™

The All Aboard Reading series is especially for beginning readers. Written by noted authors and illustrated in full color, these are books that children really and truly *want* to read—books to excite their imagination, tickle their funny bone, expand their interests, and support their feelings. With five different reading levels, All Aboard Reading lets you choose which books are most appropriate for your children and their growing abilities.

Picture Readers
Picture Readers have super-simple texts, with many nouns appearing as rebus pictures. At the end of each book are 24 flash cards—on one side is the rebus picture; on the other side is the written-out word.

First Friends
First Friends, First Readers have a super-simple text starring lovable recurring characters. Each book features two easy stories that will hold the attention of even the youngest reader while promoting an early sense of accomplishment.

Level 1
Level 1 books have very few lines per page, very large type, easy words, lots of repetition, and pictures with visual "cues" to help children figure out the words on the page.

Level 2
Level 2 books are printed in slightly smaller type than Level 1 books. The stories are more complex, but there is still lots of repetition in the text, and many pictures. The sentences are quite simple and are broken up into short lines to make reading easier.

Level 3
Level 3 books have considerably longer texts, harder words, and more complicated sentences.

All Aboard for happy reading!

Library of Congress Cataloging-in-Publication Data

Faiella, Graham.
  Whales / Graham Faiella ; illustrated by Turi MacCombie.
    p. cm. — (All aboard reading. Level 2.)
Summary: Outlines some of the facts and mysteries about whales, including the different species, what they eat, and how they breathe.
    1. Whales—Juvenile literature. [1. Whales.] I. MacCombie, Turi, ill.
  II. Title. III. Series.
  QL737.C4 F27 2002
  599.5—dc21   2002003971

ISBN 0-448-42837-7 (GB)   A B C D E F G H I J

ISBN 0-448-42600-5 (pb)   A B C D E F G H I J

ALL
ABOARD
READING™

Level 2

Grades 1-3

WITHDRAWN
Whales

By Graham Faiella
Illustrated by Turi MacCombie

Grosset & Dunlap • New York

A boat is out at sea.

The only sound is from the waves.

Swoosh! Swoosh!

Then the sailors hear something—

clicks and whirs.

The sounds grow louder and closer.

What can it be?

It is a whale—

a humpback whale.

And it is singing!

Why do humpback whales sing?

Are they talking to one another?

Maybe.

Nobody knows for sure.

It is a whale mystery.

There are almost seventy-five
different types of whales in the world.

sei (it sounds like "SAY") whale

minke (MINK-ee) whale

fin whale

sperm whale

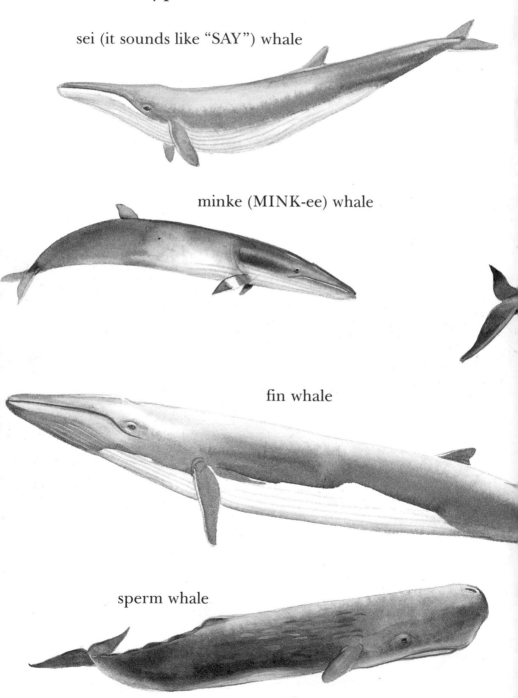

right whale

pilot whale

bowhead (BOW-head) whale

orca whale

dwarf sperm whale

gray whale

11

The blue whale is the biggest.

It is the biggest animal

in the world.

Even the biggest dinosaur

was not as big.

This is a dwarf sperm whale.

It is one

of the smallest whales.

It could almost fit in a bathtub.

Whales live in the sea.

But they are not fish!

Whales are mammals

like cats and dogs.

You are a mammal, too.

Like all mammals,
whales are born alive
from their mother.

Most fish lay eggs.

Like all mammals,

baby whales drink milk from their mother.

Some baby whales drink

50 gallons a day.

That is 800 glasses of milk!

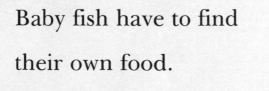

Baby fish have to find

their own food.

Their mothers do not feed them.

gill

Fish can breathe underwater.

They have gills.

Like all mammals,

whales have lungs.

They need to hold their breath

underwater.

They can hold their breath

a long time—

for two hours, sometimes!

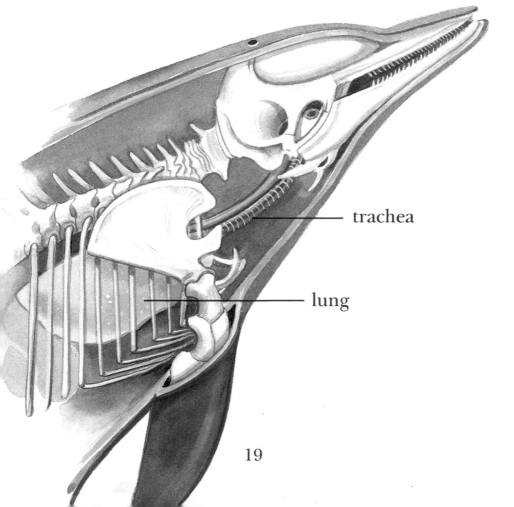

trachea

lung

19

This is a sperm whale.

It dives down deep to look for food.

And the food it most likes to eat is . . .

squid!

The sperm whale spots a giant squid.

The squid is almost

as long as the whale.

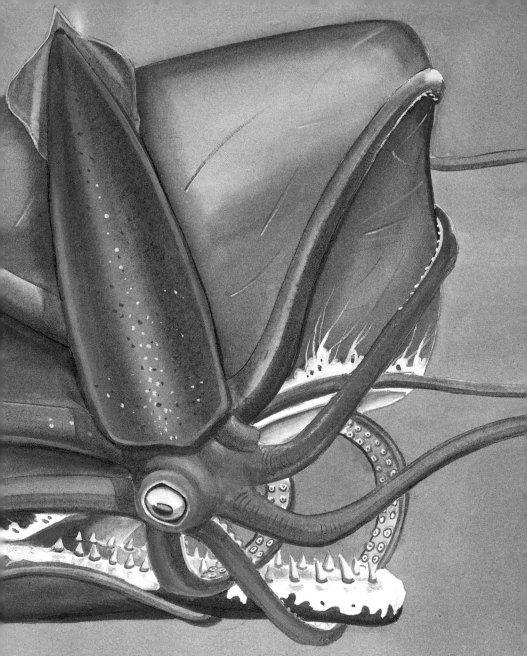

It grabs the sperm whale.

But the sperm whale bites the squid

again and again.

After a while,

the squid cannot fight anymore.

The sperm whale opens its jaws,

and eats the giant squid.

Shllllurp!

The sperm whale needs air now.

Up, up, up, it swims,

up out of the dark, deep sea.

The sperm whale comes up

right out of the water.

It breathes in air through a hole

on its head.

This is called a blowhole.

The blowhole is like a nose.

Out shoots a jet

of air and water.

Spwoosh!

This jet is called a spout.

You can tell a whale

by its spout.

The sperm whale's spout

goes off to the left.

The humpback whale has

a spout like a big bush.

A blue whale's spout goes up, up, up—

30 feet high.

Like most whales,

the orca has teeth.

It eats squid and crabs,

turtles and octopus,

and even other whales!

Some whales do <u>not</u> have teeth.

They have baleen.

Baleen is like a stringy curtain.

It hangs down in their mouth.

Gray whales have baleen.

They swim

with their mouth open.

Water flows in.

In the water are

tiny shrimp called krill.

The krill stick to the baleen.

The gray whale closes its mouth.

It spits out the water.

Spwooooosh!

Then it licks off the krill in the baleen.

Shluuurp!

A hungry whale can eat

half a ton of krill a day.

Humpbacks have baleen.

They eat krill.

But they also catch food another way.

They can blow a net of bubbles.

A school of fish gets trapped in the net.

The whale gulps down the fish.

A humpback can eat

200 pounds of fish in one gulp!

Whales go wherever
they can find food.
Some spend their whole life
in the same place.
Some kinds of whales
swim all over the ocean.

Humpbacks spend the summer

in the cold waters around

the South or North Pole.

They eat tons of krill and squid.

In the fall,

they swim

to warm waters.

They have their babies there.

They swim

back and forth

like this

every year.

NORTH
POLE

And whales can live
a pretty long time.
A humpback can live
up to 50 years.
A sperm whale can live
up to 70 years.
A fin whale can live
up to 90 years.

In all that time, whales do not sleep—

at least, not the way we do.

They rest in the water.

They nap.

They must get tired
from all that swimming
and eating . . .

. . . and jumping!

Whales jump a lot.

A whale shoots up out of the water.

Then it falls back with a huge

SPLASH!

Another whale jumps.

Ker-SPLASH!

And another!

It's a whale ballet!

Why are they jumping?

Are they showing off to other whales?

Are they getting rid of

bugs on their bodies?

Or are they just having fun?

No one knows for sure.

It is another whale mystery.